JUDY HANDWERKER

Books published by Emerald Lake Books may be ordered through booksellers or by contacting:

Emerald Lake Books
44 Green Pond Rd
Sherman, CT 06784

http://emeraldlakebooks.com
860-946-0544

ISBN: 978-0-9965674-4-2

Printed in the United States of America

Dedication

This book is lovingly dedicated to my mom, Martha
Cornelius, a beautiful and wise woman who raised my sister
and I singlehandedly when my dad died at a very young age.
She poured her whole life into us. From time to time, she
would look at me and say
"Judy, enjoy your life!"

Table of Contents

Introduction

Why write a devotional on *joy*?

We live in a time when there are sorrows and tragedies everywhere we look. If we constantly consume the news on the TV and internet, we will find ourselves zapped of the energy we need to complete our God-given assignments. Life would become a gloomy, morose existence. We are called to a high quality of life – a lifestyle of righteousness, peace and joy in the Holy Spirit. Truly, God's joy is our strength.

The Bible is replete with thoughts and expressions of joy. As we read and study, we discover that our God, our heavenly Father, sings, laughs and dances. (Zeph. 3 ☺) He takes pleasure in us and it is his pleasure to give us everything he has to enjoy and share with others. We Christians must exude this joy in our daily activities.

Years ago, as I was journaling about my struggles, the Lord inspired me to search the scriptures for reasons why I should rejoice. I compiled them and put them away. About two years ago, the inspiration resurfaced with the idea to develop a devotional.

Each day you will find a devotional filled with golden nuggets of scripture to combat every "killjoy" attack of Satan and life's circumstances. At the end of each devotional, there is a prayer to activate your faith and increase your joy.

I hope that you truly enjoy it and I pray that your life will become filled with the effervescent presence of our joyful King.

Day 1. Walking in the Light of His Glory

Blessed (happy, fortunate, to be envied) are the people who know the joyful sound [who understand and appreciate the spiritual blessings symbolized by the feasts]; they walk, O Lord, in the light and favor of Your countenance! In Your name they rejoice all the day, and in Your righteousness they are exalted.
(Ps. 89:15-16)

I will make an effort to learn how to rejoice today. We who know the lessons of joy-on-demand will always walk in the light of his glory. It is not only for Sunday mornings when we hear the choir sing our favorite song. Let's train our emotions every day to be joyful.

As the skilled violinist trains for hours to play a tune perfectly and, at a moment's notice, when asked to play, she plays beautifully because she knows how. We, as sons and daughters, must practice daily to be joyful in him.

Some days, when there are struggles, we practice minute by minute and hour by hour. We speak to ourselves in psalms and hymns, creating a melody in our heart to the Lord. And we not only have a good time, but we get to walk in his glory, and are exuberant in His majestic presence.

Miracles happen in our lives because of his glory. Doors that were once shut are opened. Resources and people are coming to our aid as we accomplish our kingdom assignments with joy. Our paths are made plain and we see clearly where we need to go.

We anticipate glorious experiences, and wonderful interventions of the supernatural become normal to us. No shadows hovering over us because the light of his countenance is upon us. We have more than enough joy to take us through the day.

"Zip-a-Dee-Doo-Dah! Zip-a-Dee-Day! My, oh my, what a wonderful day, Plenty of 'Sonshine' heading my way, Wonderful feeling, Wonderful day."

Prayer: Heavenly Father, I fellowship with you and the Son and the Holy Spirit. I embrace you, my exceeding joy. I love you. Thank you for being the Light of my Life and teaching me to walk in your glory. I look forward with great enthusiasm to the things you have planned for me.

Further Reading: Isaiah 60

Day 2. His Satisfaction of Mercy

O satisfy us with Your mercy and loving-kindness in the morning [now, before we are older], that we may rejoice and be glad all our days. **(Ps. 90:14)**

We anticipate and relish the Lord's mercies today. Mercy is an undeserved blessing from the Lord for when we miss the mark. It dries our tears and causes us to look up and look ahead with hope.

Out of the deep recesses of his love, he pours out this attribute of himself that penetrates our inner being. It releases us from the bondage of guilt and condemnation.

As we embrace this expression of love, it eases our pain and silences the vicious attacks of the accuser on our minds. I can hear the Lord saying to the evil one "They are forgiven. You have no hold on them."

As we think about the word "satisfaction," we tend only to think of contentment and pleasure, but satisfaction is also a settlement of a debt. We can truly rejoice because he has satisfied the wages of sin with the death of his Son.

What a salvation! We didn't deserve it. It was his mercy. The verdict has come in and we are free to go and sin no more.

Furthermore, his mercy gives us the courage to handle the consequences of past sins and live life to the fullest without falling into the abyss of hopelessness. We can now experience the joy of true liberty and peace.

Prayer: Heavenly Father, today I confess all of my sin and I revel in your fresh mercies. I am elated by the multitude of mercies that you have released upon my life today.

Further Reading: Lam. 3:22, Ps. 103:8

Day 3. Rejoicing in God's Thoughts toward Me

For I know the thoughts and plans that I have for you, says the Lord, thoughts and plans for welfare and peace and not for evil, to give you hope in your final outcome. **(Jer. 29:11)**

How precious and weighty also are Your thoughts to me, O God! How vast is the sum of them! **(Ps. 139:17)**

His thoughts toward us are precious, powerful and numerous. They transcend far above any negative words spoken over our lives.

Most of us at some time or other have experienced negative thoughts and heard negative words from people who tried to erode our confidence and joy. King David had his share of struggles and trials. His brothers accused him. King Saul pursued him. And his own son, Absalom, attempted to take the kingdom from him.

But what sustained David was that he drew strength and comfort from his intimate fellowship with the Lord. His knowledge of the compassionate heart of God toward him was his arsenal of hope.

Confidence and courage reigned in his heart because of the continuous barrage of positive thoughts the God of Israel had toward him. He understood that God knew him in his mother's womb and, if he found himself in a dark place, God's presence superseded that.

He declared boldly "I am wonderfully and fearfully made." Embracing this, he triumphed over the challenges he faced. Let us seize and hold on to what he says in his holy word.

Prayer: I appreciate you, Heavenly Father. I am grateful for your word and your thoughts toward me. They are truly spirit and life. I am inspired and energized to be all that you have destined me to be. I speak to my soul today, "be joyful in the One who created you, redeemed you and who loves you."

Further Reading: Ps. 40:5, Ps. 33:11

Day 4. Clothed with His Salvation and Righteousness

I will greatly rejoice in the Lord, my soul will exult in my God; for He has clothed me with the garments of salvation, He has covered me with the robe of righteousness, as a bridegroom decks himself with a garland, and as a bride adorns herself with her jewels. **(Isa. 61:10)**

God's mind for us is that we are fully clothed with peace and joy. It is no fun being naked, dirty and bruised.

As we drive through our cities, sometimes we see homeless people, dirty and barely clad. We can see the destitution and hopelessness in their eyes. Our hearts go out to them because we remember that, at one time, we were like that spiritually, but the Lord Jesus Christ paid the price so we can be clean, whole and fully dressed.

As one songwriter penned, "He has taken away my old tattered garments and has given me a robe of pure white." No more wearing the garb of shame, guilt, condemnation or low self-esteem.

It is replacement time. The garment of praise for the spirit of depression, the garment of healing for the spirit of infirmity, the garment of deliverance for the spirit of addiction, clothing of freedom from the chains of bondage, and the clothing of a sound mind from confusion.

But there is one that tops all lists, the garment of righteousness (being in right-standing with God). With this robe of righteousness, we reign in life by our savior, the Lord Jesus Christ. Let's go into our spiritual wardrobe and get royally dressed today.

Prayer: Heavenly Father, I thank you for my beautiful garments of peace and joy. I refuse to live below my royal privilege. I leave my house fully dressed today with your garment of righteousness.

Further Reading: Ps. 132:9, 16, Isa. 61: 1-3

Day 5. Safe and Secure in You

For You have been my help, and in the shadow of Your wings will I rejoice. (Ps. 63:7)

I nestle under his everlasting wings today. What a place to be at all times! He calls us to this place of love and peace and, to our surprise, we find an abundance of joy.

The Wicked One can't touch us in this haven of safety. All anxieties, calamities and fears are shut out as we make our way into this secret place.

Learning to hide under his wings is critical. In no other thing or person can we find safety and security. As the old hymn goes, "Safe and secure from all alarms" (and all calamities, dangers and snares too).

We encounter this secret place through prayer and worship. As we hide in his presence, casting all our cares upon him, we can truly relax and enjoy the journey through every storm of life.

Prayer: I refuse to be prey for the devourer today. I take refuge in you. It is so wonderful to know I can run to you and take shelter in the shadow of your wings. I jump for joy because of this access.

Further Reading: Col. 3:1-2, John 10:29, Ps. 91:1

Day 6. Delighting in the Abundance of Peace

*But the meek [in the end] shall inherit the earth and shall
delight themselves in the abundance of peace.*
(Ps. 37:11)

Who delights themselves in the abundance of peace? The
meek! They are those who are humble and lowly in heart
with strength under control.

We live in a world that equates meekness with weakness.
The proud declares nasty things fearlessly and unabashed.
They seem to be successful, but there is no peace for them.

We have to constantly renew our minds with the mind of the
Master, who humbled himself to death on the cross.

News of turmoil, calamity, distress and sorrow billow
through the various networks. Most individuals are feverishly
looking for something to calm their anxious souls, but
unfortunately they are seeking solace and peace in all the
wrong places. It is so refreshing that, as we humble ourselves
before God, we are blessed with an abundance of peace.

Prayer: I humble myself today under your mighty hand and as a child I revel in the superfluity of peace. Thank you, Lord, for the ever-increasing flow. I go out with peace today and I anticipate questions about you, the Prince of Peace, living in me.

Day 7. Expressing the Joy of Faith

Though the fig tree does not blossom and there is no fruit on the vines, [though] the product of the olive fails and the fields yield no food, though the flock is cut off from the fold and there are no cattle in the stalls, Yet I will rejoice in the Lord; I will exult in the [victorious] God of my salvation! The Lord God is my Strength, my personal bravery, and my invincible army; He makes my feet like hinds' feet and will make me to walk [not to stand still in terror, but to walk] and make [spiritual] progress upon my high places [of trouble, suffering, or responsibility]! (**Hab. 3:17-19**)

Learning to express good things with joy, even when the circumstances or situation are not favorable; this is a walk of faith. We can't do this on our own. He is our strength and courage.

As we allow ourselves to be trained in the Lord's boot camp, we always come out triumphant and strengthened.

The time that we spend in this boot camp is not always comfortable. It might be a financial challenge… We cry to the Lord, saying we have given our tithes and offerings, but where is the return?

He is silent. It is at this time that we truly have to be weaned from looking at the natural and draw sustenance from heaven (the supernatural). We enter into another level of trust, a different walk, from whining to truly dining on his promises.

Habakkuk expressed this bold declaration when there wasn't any evidence of good in the land. There was no visible sign of productivity, but he said "I will rejoice in him."

The bottom line is enjoying God for who he is, not only for the benefits and blessings that he gives. The present non-productivity doesn't move me, but I choose to enjoy my Savior in these trying times because they don't last forever.

Jesus, you are my strength, my prosperity and my deliverer. Why shouldn't I rejoice?

Prayer: Heavenly Father, I make a conscious effort to enjoy you today in spite of the circumstances, what I see or hear. You are my strength, personal bravery and invincible army.

Day 8. The Joy of Victory

Hannah prayed, and said, My heart exults and triumphs in the Lord; my horn (my strength) is lifted up in the Lord. My mouth is no longer silent, for it is opened wide over my enemies, because I rejoice in Your salvation. **(1 Sam. 2:1)**

But thanks be to God, Who in Christ always leads us in triumph [as trophies of Christ's victory] and through us spreads and makes evident the fragrance of the knowledge of God everywhere. **(2 Cor. 2:14)**

Victory is our portion, says the redeemed. Could you imagine being picked on by a bully and as this mean person was about to land their first punch on you, a prizefighter stepped in and floored them? You would shout out with a voice of triumph and thank your hero.

It is the same with our salvation. The Lord Jesus Christ gave Satan a knockout punch so that we can live a victorious life. Our redemption was purchased at a very high price, and it is our responsibility and privilege to take the victory.

Where do we need victory today? It might be saying "no" to peer pressure, facing foreclosure, favor in a court case, a health issue… Whatever the challenge we encounter, we are guaranteed victory. Yet, it takes faith on our part to experience that victory.

As we meditate on 2 Cor 2:14, the Holy Spirit prompts us to cast down a defeatist mindset, points out a strategy for our situation, and encourages us to embrace victory.

A great example of this is when Moses and the children of Israel came out of Egypt. After travelling for three days without water, they encountered bitter waters. They needed another victory. Moses prayed to the Lord and he gave him the answer. He showed him a tree to put into the water, which made it sweet.

When we take a stand for victory, we are making a strong declaration against the enemy of our soul. We must refuse to back down and then we win despite how the situation looks. Our confession of faith is big and bold. Everything, everyone and every situation must bow to his rule in our lives.

Prayer: Heavenly Father, I sing for joy to you. The birds can't sing for me, nor the angels, for so great a salvation you have wrought for me. My mouth is open wide for you to fill it with all of the great things you are doing in my life and that you are about to do. I want to experience your victory today. Open my eyes to new ways of doing things and the strategies to bring victory to my situation.

Further Reading: Rom. 8:37, 1 John 5:4, Exod. 15:23-25

Day 9. What a Pleasure Being Able to Come to the Father Face-to-Face

Let us then fearlessly and confidently and boldly draw near to the throne of grace (the throne of God's unmerited favor to us sinners), that we may receive mercy [for our failures] and find grace to help in good time for every need [appropriate help and well-timed help, coming just when we need it]. (Heb. 4:16)

We live in the age of technology, where it is rare to hear a live human's voice when we call a company to make a payment or get some information. Or we must go through gatekeepers before we can speak to a manager or supervisor.

It is not so with my heavenly Father. I rejoice this morning that, by the blood of Jesus, I am able to come boldly before the throne of grace and be face-to-face having beautiful conversations; to know that I don't have to depend on any human third party, but as I come in the precious name of Jesus, I am guaranteed an audience with the King of Kings and Lord of Lords.

I gain strength and momentum from His abundant grace to run this race. Gazing in his wonderful face, I am moved from one level of glory to another. When Moses came down from the mount after forty days with the Lord, his face gleamed with his presence. Hallelujah!

Prayer: Heavenly Father, I wait in your presence this morning. I am captivated by you. I radiate your glory today.

Day 10. Pure Delight in His Word

The precepts of the Lord are right, rejoicing the heart; the commandment of the Lord is pure and bright, enlightening the eyes. The [reverent] fear of the Lord is clean, enduring forever; the ordinances of the Lord are true and righteous altogether. More to be desired are they than gold, even than much fine gold; they are sweeter also than honey and drippings from the honeycomb. (Ps. 19:8-10)

We hear stories sometimes of people buying items from a tag or garage sale for pennies, only to realize later that the item they bought is worth a lot of money. They are ecstatic at the find.

We also love to watch the "Antique Road Show" to see the expression on an individual's face when the appraiser tells her that the painting or a piece of furniture is one of the few that the artist created and it's worth thousands of dollars. Her face lights up with pure delight.

In the Word of our God, as we read, study and meditate, we discover golden nuggets of inspiration that can change our lives spiritually, mentally and emotionally. These nuggets not only bring change in our personal lives, but this deposit of sweetness from heaven touches the lives of people we meet on a daily basis. They are priceless!

Prayer: Today, I look for and receive joy in the right place, your Word. I reject the temptation to search for pleasure in the wrong places.

Further Reading: Ps. 119:16, 24, 62

Day 11. Rejoicing for Good Behavior and a Pure Conscience

It is a reason for pride and exultation to which our conscience testifies that we have conducted ourselves in the world [generally] and especially toward you, with devout and pure motives and godly sincerity, not in fleshly wisdom but by the grace of God (the unmerited favor and merciful kindness by which God, exerting His holy influence upon souls, turns them to Christ, and keeps, strengthens, and increases them in Christian virtues). (2 Cor. 1:12)

In a world where bad behavior is heralded, we choose to conduct ourselves in the way of the Master, living life with a clear conscience, purity in heart and not self-seeking.

Someone said "don't do what you wouldn't want to see on the front page of the newspaper." How true it is for us as Christians, because we are called to a higher standard of living and answer to a higher authority. The Lord Jesus said, on Judgment Day some things that were said in private would be shouted from the rooftop. We only want to hear good things broadcasted on that day.

Although David was a man after God's own heart, he modeled some bad behavior in his time. He committed adultery, lied and killed, which brought him much sorrow. We are people after God's own heart and we must purposefully give him pleasure in our hearts.

Wouldn't it be wonderful for him to say to the enemy "Have you seen my servant, _____? Her conduct is impeccable," and to say "This is my daughter, in whom I am well-pleased."

Our good behavior pleases the Father and encourages those around us who are desperately looking for godly examples.

Prayer: Heavenly Father, I yield myself to walk perfectly before you. I am letting my light shine before men so they can glorify you. Holy Spirit, help me to constantly judge myself and repent so I can go to another stage of glory in my walk with you.

Further Reading: Ps. 50:23, 1 Tim. 3:15, 2 Tim. 1:3, Rom. 12:1-2, 3 John 3

Day 12. Thy Comforts Delight My Soul

In the multitude of my [anxious] thoughts within me, Your comforts cheer and delight my soul! **(Ps. 94:19)**

As the songwriter pens, "when I think of the goodness of Jesus and all that he has done for me, my soul cries out 'Hallelujah! Praise God for saving me.'"

I am so blessed because of every good thing he has bestowed upon me. As I let my mind feast on these things, they comfort my soul. I refuse to be discouraged, sad or mad. I am training in the school of heavenly joy. New lessons I am receiving every day.

There are so many comforts in knowing our Lord. They can't be numbered. One of the comforts is knowing that he is my good Shepherd. He makes me to lie down in green pastures. Even his chastening (his rod) comforts me.

It is heartwarming to know that I am his child. We are not left to go our own way or do our own thing, which leads to destruction. He loves us so much that even when we go the wrong way, he searches for us to bring us back to his presence.

Prayer: Lord, I draw on your comforts today. I need you every day, every moment. I thank you for causing my soul to be joyful in your compassions and comforts. They are fresh every morning. They are beyond anything I can comprehend.

Further Reading: Ps. 23:4, Ps. 40:5, Ps. 139:17, Jer. 29:11

Day 13. The Lord Is My Defense

But let all those who take refuge and put their trust in You rejoice; let them ever sing and shout for joy, because You make a covering over them and defend them; let those also who love Your name be joyful in You and be in high spirits.
(Ps. 5:11)

The Presidents of United States are guarded by the Secret Service. They protect them from being assassinated, but unfortunately in some cases the Secret Service agents were not able defend them.

Some celebrities have numerous bodyguards and still they are not shielded from the paparazzi and crazy fans.

Who do we have? We have the King of Kings and the Lord of Lords. A mighty warrior is watching over us. As the songwriter rightly penned, "His eyes are on the sparrow and I know he watches over me." I shall not be afraid because you, the Almighty God, protect me.

I can remember many occasions where the Lord has been my defense. One time, he protected me on a short-term missionary trip in Kenya. I was under a heavy spiritual attack. I thought I might die there. Another time he saved me from being run over in the street.

I can go on and on. No more quiet praise for you, Lord. I give loud praise to you before I leave my house today. Glory! You encircle my life with favor as a shield. I acknowledge that you are my tower of refuge.

Prayer: Heavenly Father, I thank you for protecting my life today and giving me your Heavenly escorts (angels).

Further Reading: Ps. 7:10, Ps. 89:18, Ps. 94:22

Day 14. Favoring Your Righteous Cause

Let those who favor my righteous cause and have pleasure in my uprightness shout for joy and be glad and say continually, Let the Lord be magnified, Who takes pleasure in the prosperity of His servant.

(Ps. 35:27)

In this busy world, there are so many things fighting for our attention; relationships, work, businesses, toys, pleasures, cares... We must fight back and follow God's agenda because it pleases our heavenly Father, and in doing his will we find true fulfillment and joy.

We were created for his pleasure. Are we making and taking the time to look after the needy, setting the captives free, healing the broken-hearted? Are we sensitive to the things that are dear to the Father's heart?

We must say to ourselves and others, "I must be busy about my Father's business." The Lord Jesus was here on earth for thirty-three years, doing His work for three and half years. He got the job done because his total focus was doing only what his Father told him to do and say.

Prayer: Holy Spirit, cause me to be sensitive today to your causes. Give me eyes to see the hurting and those to whom you will have me say a kind word, minister the gospel, or give finances. Most of all, I pray for those you would put on my heart. Gird me with your militancy to stand for righteousness.

Further Reading: Jer. 22:15-16, Isa. 61:1-2, Matt. 6:33

Day 15. Being a Helper of Someone's Joy

Not that we have dominion [over you] and lord it over your
faith, but [rather that we work with you as] fellow laborers
[to promote] your joy, for in [your] faith (in your strong and
welcome conviction or belief that Jesus is the Messiah,
through Whom we obtain eternal salvation in the kingdom of
God) you stand firm.
(2 Cor. 1:24)

We as believers have to constantly renew our minds and
remember to love one another as we love ourselves. The
promotion of self has taken on an inordinate amount of
attention.

Today, our focus is not only to make myself happy, for this is
fleeting. What can I do to help bring about someone else's
joy?

Joy is spiritual and heavenly, so I have to ask the Father how
I can help those around me and those who come across my
path or within my influence to increase their joy.

We can encourage them to be obedient to the heavenly call,
walk in the truth, have unpretentious love for one another,
and be of the same mind as the Father. Or we can do an act of
kindness, such as paying a bill for a struggling family,

visiting an acquaintance in the hospital, or making time to talk to someone who lives alone.

Prayer: Holy Spirit, show me whose joy I can increase today. Give me your creativity and wisdom for how to influence their lives. Let your oil of joy flow freely through me today, so its fragrance will attract and captivate others to rejoice before you as never before. Let my life be a mirror of your joy. I love you!

Further Reading: Phil. 2:2, 2 Thess. 1:11

Day 16. Joy in the Atonement

*Not only so, but we also rejoice and exultingly glory in God
[in His love and perfection] through our Lord Jesus Christ,
through Whom we have now received and enjoy [our]
reconciliation.* **(Rom. 5:11)**

Atonement is a big word that simply means "reconciliation."
We take pleasure in him by whom we have received
reconciliation. One songwriter says, "when I think of the
goodness of Jesus and all that he has done for me, my soul
cries out 'Thank God for saving me.'"

Let's meditate on what that means to us. Jesus' precious
blood, not the blood of goats and bulls, has paid the price for
you and for me. I was once a sinner. How can I not rejoice in
him who made it possible for me to come into a relationship
with Almighty God that I can call him "Daddy?"

This atonement has given the abundance of grace. It is so
deep and powerful that, because of it, I have a brand new
spirit. My conscience is constantly cleansed. All of my sins
are forgiven.

Even if everything around me is chaotic, I will rejoice over
what he has done for me. I will not neglect my relationship
and connection with him today.

Prayer: Thank you for loving me so much that you gave your Son to die for me. Lord Jesus, I appreciate your precious blood that was shed for me. I value the bond that sacrifice restored.

Day 17. Rejoice that the Gospel Is Being Preached

But what does it matter, so long as either way, whether in pretense [for personal ends] or in all honesty [for the furtherance of the Truth], Christ is being proclaimed? And in that I [now] rejoice, yes, and I shall rejoice [hereafter] also.
(Phil. 1:18)

Can we rejoice when the gospel is being preached in pretense? Yes, we can and should. Paul was in prison when he wrote this epistle to the Philippians. He could have been very angry or sorrowful to hear the gospel being misrepresented at times, but instead he chose to rejoice.

Let's rejoice that the gospel is reaching people groups throughout the world, even in those areas that have never heard it before. Let's rejoice when Christianity gets bad press through the media. It may not make sense, but we will rejoice. The gospel does not lose its power through bad press. It is still powerful.

The kingdom of our God rules over all. The Good News is getting out.

Prayer: Holy Spirit, help me to rejoice and not be upset when people misrepresent the gospel. My Jesus lives and lives are being changed every day.

Day 18. We Are Getting Ready

Let us rejoice and shout for joy [exulting and triumphant]!
Let us celebrate and ascribe to Him glory and honor, for the
marriage of the Lamb [at last] has come, and His bride has
prepared herself.
(Rev. 19:7)

Signs of the times are everywhere. We are not moved by the
gloomy forecast. Prophecies in the Bible forewarn us that
these things would come. We look forward with anticipation
to the coming of the King in the same way that a bride is
enthusiastic about her wedding day and prepares extensively.

We, as the Body of Christ, are having a great time getting
ready. We are sending out invitations to the masses to repent.
We are making sure that we have extra oil with our vessels
and are looking for his appearing at any time.

There is a quiet satisfaction and joy when we know we are
busy about our Father's business. In our individual lives, we
surrender to the Holy Spirit's prompting to clean up anything
that grieves him and allow him to perfect everything
concerning our lives.

Prayer: Heavenly Father, I keep my eyes on you at all times. Holy Spirit, show me anything that does not give you pleasure and help me to be busy about my heavenly Father's business. I choose to keep myself in state of readiness for my bridegroom, Jesus Christ.

Day 19. Joy Is the Bucket

Behold, God, my salvation! I will trust and not be afraid, for the Lord God is my strength and song; yes, He has become my salvation. Therefore with joy will you draw water from the wells of salvation.
(Isa. 12:2-3)

Let's picture years ago, back when there was no plumbing, indoors or out, and you had to get water from a well. The well is deep and the only access to the abundance of fresh water is a wooden bucket on a rope. We don't hesitate. We immediately use the receptacle, the bucket, to draw the water we need for the necessities of our day-to-day living.

It is the same in our spiritual life. Every day, we have needs that only can be met from our spiritual wells. Joy is our receptacle, "our bucket," to draw from this magnificent salvation we have received through our Lord Jesus Christ. This bucket is only found in his presence.

We enter the presence of our King with love songs of worship and praise. Before we know it, we are having a praise party. There is a buffet table with lots of goodies. Next to the goodies is our bucket of "joy." As we pick up joy, we are energized to feast on all the goodies of our salvation:

faith, protection, provision and freedom from fear just to name a few.

Our salvation package allows us to draw healing, deliverance, grace and many other great things for ourselves.

Prayer: Heavenly Father, I take joy in your presence this day. With this bucket, I draw from your wells of salvation to live my life victoriously. I refuse to fall for the Evil One's tactics of condemnation, guilt and fear. I love you. You are truly awesome.

Further Reading: John 7:38, 1 Cor. 1:30

Day 20. Praying with Joy

*In every prayer of mine I always make my entreaty and
petition for you all with joy (delight).* **(Phil. 1:4)**

As we read through the Pauline epistles, there is a common
thread flowing through the fabric of his writing. It is the love
for the brethren. This love propelled him to be constantly in
prayer for the people in the churches he birthed.

Even in the Roman prison, his focus was on the believers on
the outside. He was thanking God for the Christians of
Philippi; a perfect model to follow. With pleasure, we should
be presenting members of the body to the Father.

At times, I do not present some brethren with joy because of
the frailty of their humanity and what I have experienced
from them. How can I turn this displeasure to pleasure in my
prayers?

What comes to mind is Hebrews 12:2, the Lord Jesus "for the
joy that was set before him, endured the cross." Through his
grace and mercy, I am able to foresee the outcome of my
prayers especially for those who have offended me.

As I release the disgust of the offense and truly pray for the
perfecting of that individual, I expect my prayers will be

answered. I expect sincerity in place of superficiality and manipulation, humility instead of pride.

I am beginning to see from God's perspective. He looks at the outcome. He is seeing what I am becoming, so therefore I see what that certain individual is becoming.

Prayer: Heavenly Father, help me to love as you love, so I can truly pray for all my brethren with joy.

Further Reading: Rom. 1:8, Eph. 1:16, Col. 1:3

Day 21. He Is Rejoicing Over Me

The Lord your God is in the midst of you, a Mighty One, a Savior [Who saves]! He will rejoice over you with joy; He will rest [in silent satisfaction] and in His love He will be silent and make no mention [of past sins, or even recall them]; He will exult over you with singing. I will gather those belonging to you [those Israelites in captivity] who yearn and grieve for the solemn assembly [and the festivals], on whom [their exile and inability to attend services at Jerusalem have brought derision and] the reproach of it is a burden. (**Zeph. 3:17-18**)

This passage of scripture is one of the most exciting, radical revelations of a loving God. It tells us so much of who he is and his ardent love for us. He is not an angry or moody person as some define him to be. He is passionate. This passion for us is seen in his movements. He is dancing and singing over us.

The Hebrew word for joy in this verse is "guwl," which means to spin under the influence of violent emotion. Envision the Lord doing pirouettes because of us.

Some believe that dancing doesn't belong in our church services. Our God is full of movement, expression and creativity. We cannot keep him in a box.

As he dances and sings over us, he is releasing joy upon us and beckons us to dance and sing with him. For this reason, he invites us to come into his presence with singing. There is nothing dull or boring about our creator and Heavenly Father. He is calling us to move to the heavenly rhythm and see miracles in our lives.

Prayer: I acknowledge your singing and dancing over me. I dance with you today.

Day 22. Doing His Pleasure Gives Us Pleasure

If you turn away your foot from [traveling unduly on] the Sabbath, from doing your own pleasure on My holy day, and call the Sabbath a [spiritual] delight, the holy day of the Lord honorable, and honor Him and it, not going your own way or seeking or finding your own pleasure or speaking with your own [idle] words.
(Isa. 58:13)

We live in a hedonistic society where a lot is centered around living to be happy and going after the latest thrill. People live for the next exotic vacation, endless partying, and loving pleasure more than God. Self-denial and living for the greater good is often relegated to the back seat.

We must remember that we are disciples of the Lord Jesus. He ministered on earth for three years so that we could see clearly how he was fully connected to the Father and did nothing on his own. He said that his "food was to do the will of him who sent me and to finish his work."

The Lord warns us about the danger of overindulgence in earthly pleasures because the Day of the Lord would be a snare to the inhabitants of the earth, but that should not be our portion. Our heavenly Father is not a party pooper, but gives us freely all things to enjoy (1 Tim. 6:17).

His whole intent is that we enjoy life and live life to the fullest. We were created for his pleasure (Rev. 4:11) and when we do his pleasure we really enjoy life to the maximum.

In Isa. 58, he drops a few hints. No self-centeredness. When we fast, it's not to exude our own righteousness. As we do and speak only what the Father inspires us to do, we will begin to celebrate in him. We will do things that last, such as affecting generations and building up wrecked lives.

Prayer: Heavenly Father, I choose to do your pleasure today. Open up my eyes to anything that I am doing that does not give you pleasure and that is not within your will. I see myself today as a restorer and builder.

Further Reading: Luke 21:34

Day 23. Living as a Kingdom Citizen

[After all] the kingdom of God is not a matter of [getting the] food and drink [one likes], but instead it is righteousness (that state which makes a person acceptable to God) and [heart] peace and joy in the Holy Spirit. **(Rom. 14:17)**

The kingdom of God is not meat and drink, but righteousness, peace and joy in the Holy Spirit. As we journey through life here on earth, we have to remember this is not our final destination. We must subject ourselves to the full rule of the kingdom of God.

The Lord made it very simple for us to follow. The dictates of kingdom are righteousness, peace and joy in the Holy Spirit. As true Christians, we pursue righteousness and peace, but at times we forget to allow the joy of the Lord to invade our situations and circumstances.

The joy of the Lord gives us the energy to run the race with patience and to overcome every obstacle along the path. The Lord is our exceeding joy and he beckons us daily to linger long enough in his presence to be saturated with himself. This enables us to face the little annoyances of life without getting angry, irritable and fretful.

Joy empowers us against the enemy of our soul. He endeavors to steal the pleasure of serving the Lord. He is a great illusionist and uses trickery and theatrics to hide the good things the Lord is doing in our lives. He makes disappointments and setbacks seem so big that we think we cannot overcome them.

But the joy of the Lord is our strength to leap over walls of opposition and run through the troops of discouragement.

Prayer: Heavenly Father, I linger in your presence this morning. Saturate me with yourself. You are my exceeding joy. I allow your nature of joy to go deep down in my spirit. Thank you for filling me up to overflowing. By your Holy Spirit, I have enough to share.

Further Reading: Phil. 3:20

Day 24. ...Enter into the Joy of the Lord

For it is like a man who was about to take a long journey, and he called his servants together and entrusted them with his property. To one he gave five talents [probably about $5,000], to another two, to another one—to each in proportion to his own personal ability. Then he departed and left the country. He who had received the five talents went at once and traded with them, and he gained five talents more. And likewise he who had received the two talents—he also gained two talents more. But he who had received the one talent went and dug a hole in the ground and hid his master's money. Now after a long time the master of those servants returned and settled accounts with them. And he who had received the five talents came and brought him five more, saying, Master, you entrusted to me five talents; see, here I have gained five talents more. His master said to him, Well done, you upright (honorable, admirable) and faithful servant! You have been faithful and trustworthy over a little; I will put you in charge of much. Enter into and share the joy (the delight, the blessedness) which your master enjoys. And he also who had the two talents came forward, saying, Master, you entrusted two talents to me; here I have gained two talents more.
(Matt. 25:14-22)

Our God is in the investment business. Actually, he is the original Investment Banker. He has invested in each of his children and expects a return on the talents he gave us.

As we observe in this parable, the two wise stewards, who made a profit for their Lord, not only were promoted from being a leader of few to being a leader over many, they received a bonus of joy. To those with the five talents and two talents who double their return, he said to them "Enter into the joy of the Lord."

What do we have in our hands? We must use it up or trade it, so at the end of the day we bring in a good return on investment for our Lord. Sometimes we get so busy looking at others, thinking the grass is greener on the other side, we forget to appreciate what God has given us.

We have both spiritual gifts and natural talents that can bless many and give glory to our King as we exercise and execute them. A good example is of a mother who had a child. This child was constantly breaking her bones. The mother came up with an idea to make colorful casts. Out of a negative situation, she drew upon her artistic talent to bring joy to her child and made a business for herself.

There is a favorite line for the Capital One commercial "What do you have in your wallet?" Let us ask ourselves today "What are my God-given talents? What are my spiritual gifts?" And let us do great things for the Lord and hear him say "Well done! Enter into my joy."

Prayer: Heavenly Father, I thank you for the gifts and talents you have given me. I choose to exercise them so you can get an enormous return on your investment in me. I appreciate your faith in me, in the Lord Jesus' Name. Amen!

Day 25. Rejoice Because Our God Is a Righteous Judge

[After all] what kind of glory [is there in it] if, when you do wrong and are punished for it, you take it patiently? But if you bear patiently with suffering [which results] when you do right and that is undeserved, it is acceptable and pleasing to God. For even to this were you called [it is inseparable from your vocation]. For Christ also suffered for you, leaving you [His personal] example, so that you should follow in His footsteps. **(1 Pet. 2:20-21)**

Have you ever thought that some people have done some bad things and gotten away with it? We might have been unjustly passed over for a promotion by an employer, lied about or have done good to some people, but they in turn treated us poorly. Instead of getting discouraged or bitter, we model the attitude of our Lord Jesus. He was reviled, but committed himself to him who judges rightly.

It is so important to know the different characteristics of our Lord. We must not only know him as our Savior, our Good Shepherd and Lover of our souls, but also as the Righteous Judge. When we find ourselves in certain unjust situations, we must turn our eyes to him, give ourselves to him and let him deal with the persons involved.

We rejoice that he is righteous and that he cannot be bought. As we do this, there is a peace that passes all understanding that floods our souls and joy accompanies it. There will be no room for discouragement and bitterness, but instead the fruit of forgiveness is harvested in our lives. The joy of the Lord energizes us to keep on loving and giving.

Prayer: Heavenly Father, I choose to rejoice in this unjust situation knowing that you are a Righteous Judge. I refuse to take matters into my own hands. I trust you to handle this for me. I am happy and excited that you are working out all things for my good.

Further Reading: Ps. 67:4

Day 26. Everything that Was Contrary to Me Was Nailed to the Cross

Having cancelled and blotted out and wiped away the handwriting of the note (bond) with its legal decrees and demands which was in force and stood against us (hostile to us). This [note with its regulations, decrees, and demands] He set aside and cleared [a]completely out of our way by nailing it to [His] cross. [God] disarmed the principalities and powers that were ranged against us and made a bold display and public example of them, in triumphing over them in Him and in it [the cross].
(Col. 2:14-15)

What the Lord Jesus Christ did for us on the cross is so enormous. When we received him as our Savior, our first thoughts were that we were free from the punishment of sin. We have peace with God and we are no longer sentenced to a lost eternity.

But as we grow in him, we discover the abundance of so great a salvation. There are so many layers that when we dig deep by obeying his word, we find a part of our salvation that was hidden.

Today, we are seeing that everything that was unfavorable, antagonistic and opposed to us, he nailed to the cross. We can now vaguely understand how weighty the cross was, though we could not fully understand it with our finite minds.

The law and its commandments justly condemned us when we missed the mark, but we have found grace in the sight of the Almighty God.

The apostle John described this perfectly. The law came by Moses, but grace and truth came by the Lord Jesus. There is no more guilt, shame or condemnation. Today, we are free to live an abundant life with grace. This is truly a reason to rejoice. We have liberty.

Prayer: Lord Jesus, I thank you for your sacrifice for me on the cross of Calvary. I realize the importance of you removing everything that was against me, generational curses, guilt, sorrows, shame and the whole "kit and caboodle."

Day 27. Embracing Godly Wisdom Delights
Our Heavenly Father

*In Him all the treasures of [divine] wisdom (comprehensive
insight into the ways and purposes of God) and [all the
riches of spiritual] knowledge and enlightenment are stored
up and lie hidden.* **(Col. 2:3)**

We hold fast to godly wisdom today. The Lord Jesus Christ
is our wisdom and we cling to him, allowing him to help us
in our decision-making and life choices that would give glory
to our heavenly Father. He rewards us who seek diligently to
put him first in all that we do.

It is important that we don't go by what we see or hear. We
should not be so caught up in our intellectualism that we
refuse to hear his gentle prodding. Let's be his true disciples,
who only do what our Father tells us.

When we please the Father in walking wisely, heaven backs
us up and he makes even our enemies to be at peace with us.
A good example of this is David being pursued by King Saul.
He handled himself more wisely. David didn't take matters in
his own hands. In the end, God protected David and he was
made king.

What we do matters. Our choices affect generations and eternity.

Prayer: Heavenly Father, by your grace, we choose to operate with godly wisdom. You said that if we lack it, we can ask for it. Today, show me if I lack wisdom in any area of my life. I ask you to flood me with it. I embrace you, Lord Jesus. You are mine.

Further Reading: Ps. 51:6, Eccl. 10:10

Day 28. Rejoicing in His Love

Draw me! We will run after you! The king brings me into his apartments! We will be glad and rejoice in you! We will recall [when we were favored with] your love, more fragrant than wine. The upright [are not offended at your choice, but sincerely] love you. He brought me to the banqueting house, and his banner over me was love [for love waved as a protecting and comforting banner over my head when I was near him]. Sustain me with raisins, refresh me with apples, for I am sick with love. He made its posts of silver, its back of gold, its seat of purple, the inside of it lovingly and intricately wrought in needlework by the daughters of Jerusalem. **(Song of Sol. 1:4, 2:4-5, 3:10)**

As I write this section on rejoicing in his love, I hear the words of this song, "He loves me, He loves me and it is a brand new story."

Today I meditate on how much God loves me. We read in his Word that God loved us so much that he gave his only unique Son, the Lord Jesus, to die for us. But do I really know the depths of his love?

At various times in our lives, we get fearful, but the Word says that "there is no fear in perfect love." I remember back in 2000, I was on a short mission's trip in Kenya and I came under a spiritual and physical attack.

No one around me understood what was going on with me. I feared that I was going to die in that foreign land. I didn't feel his presence and I forgot that he loves me so much. He was there with me all along. Toward the end of the trip, he sent a dear man of God to pray for me. No condemnation.

I got sleep that night after many sleepless nights. The Lord brought me safely home to my husband. What I learned from that experience is that I must trust in his love. No one loves me as much as he does.

The Lord desires that we know this deep down in our hearts. This knowledge must go beyond a mere head knowledge of the scriptures. His love should embolden, comfort and strengthen us. Our God is the lover of our souls.

Prayer: Heavenly Father, I am happy that you have brought me to your banquet table. Most of all, your banner (your authority) over me is your love. I appreciate your love. I cherish your love and bask in your love. I desire that the knowledge of your love for me goes deep in me, so that when I encounter any challenge, I will never forget that I am more than a conqueror through you who loved me.

Further Reading: Rom. 8:37-38, 1 John 4:18

Day 29. My Glory and the Lifter of My Head

But You, O Lord, are a shield for me, my glory, and the lifter
of my head. **(Ps. 3:3)**

One thing have I asked of the Lord, that will I seek, inquire
for, and [insistently] require: that I may dwell in the house of
the Lord [in His presence] all the days of my life, to behold
and gaze upon the beauty [the sweet attractiveness and the
delightful loveliness] of the Lord and to meditate, consider,
and inquire in His temple. **(Ps. 27:4)**

We live in a time when there are many motivational
speakers, life coaches, health gurus and self-help books that
seek to encourage us to be our best and have a positive
outlook in life. These sources of stimuli have some ability to
spur us to action and to respond optimistically. They might
even pull us out of the doldrums temporarily. However, these
temporary fixes and band-aids can hardly compare to the
ultimate "picker-upper" we believers have in our Creator
God.

When King David sang this psalm to the Lord, he was
troubled by his son, Absalom's, rebellion; a son whom he
loved so much that at his son's death David uttered these
words, "Absalom, Absalom, I wished it was me."

Lured with deception, the hearts of the people turned away from David and toward Absalom. David looked to the Lord's transcendent beauty to raise him up to a place of exaltation far above these hurtful events. David had learned through fellowship with his God how to ascend through praise and worship into the holy presence of the Lord.

As he ascended, he was hidden in the secret place of the Most High and elevated to a position that "his head was lifted above his enemies." David's relationship with the Lord enabled him to turn the lemons of his life experiences into the most delicious lemonade, from which we can learn many lessons.

Through his challenges, he triumphed. Nothing can beat the presence of the Lord to give us exuberance, vitality and cheerfulness.

Prayer: Heavenly Father, in you I live, move and have my being. I refuse discouragement and I look to you, the Fountain of Life, to be recharged and revitalized.

Day 30. He Is the Shield of Our Help and the Sword of Our Excellency

Happy are you, O Israel, and blessing is yours! Who is like you, a people saved by the Lord, the Shield of your help, the Sword that exalts you! Your enemies shall come fawning and cringing, and submit feigned obedience to you, and you shall march on their high places. (**Deut. 33:29**)

Today, we hear a lot about weapons of mass destruction and many are concerned that they don't fall into the wrong hands. But I am overjoyed to know that I too have weapons of mass destruction against the enemy of my soul when I worship my great and mighty God. There is no one like him or above him. He is a mighty warrior and my invincible army.

I am encouraged that he fights for me. I remember an old song that says "Victory is mine if I let the Lord fight my battles."

We can never be outnumbered. When the children of Israel under the reign of King Jehoshaphat faced a formidable enemy, they were instructed to strategically put the worship team in the forefront. As they began to sing praises, the Lord of Hosts released the weapons of mass destruction against their enemies and they returned home with joy.

What are some of your enemies today? Doubt, fear, discouragement, heaviness? Let's start a praise party to the Lord of Hosts and watch him destroy these enemies.

Prayer: Lord of Hosts, I praise you. I exalt your name. Your kingdom reigns over all. I magnify you. You are victorious over my enemies. You are beautiful in holiness. I am more than a conqueror because of you.

Further Reading: Ex. 15, 2 Chron. 20:1-27, Rev. 12:10-11

Day 31. A Merry Heart Does Good Like a Medicine...

A happy heart is good medicine and a cheerful mind works healing, but a broken spirit dries up the bones. (**Prov. 17:22**)

At destruction and famine you shall laugh, neither shall you be afraid of the living creatures of the earth.
(**Job 5:22**)

Joy is not only good for our spiritual and emotional health, but also for our physical health. The Lord is interested in every area of our life and desires us to be whole. He uses joy to counteract the toxins of life, such as stress.

Just think! Enjoying the pleasures of his presence will heal me. Dr Michael Miller, the Director of the Center for Preventive Cardiology at the University of Maryland, and his team of researchers found out that laughter protects the heart. They noted that laughter and a sense of humor can prevent a heart attack. So in addition to eating a healthy diet, exercise and not smoking, they encouraged hearty laughter a couple of times a day.

When the Lord tells us to laugh at the negative things in life, we should go ahead and enjoy ourselves. Let the healing begin. No more mopey faces. Enjoy a belly laugh! Ha! Ha! Ha!

Prayer: Lord, I thank you for joy today. I laugh today at everything that is trying to get me down. I wait in your presence and allow the rivers of your pleasure to flow through my spirit, soul and body.

About the Author

Judy Handwerker is a committed Christian who ardently loves the Word of God.

She is an ordained minister of the gospel and has served in the local church as a teacher and Praise dance minister. She has taught praise and worship dance to children, teenagers and adults. She continues to minister in "Prophetic Worship" dance in New York and Connecticut.

She is the owner of Judy Global Wholeness, LLC dba as Wonderfully Whole and KidsFit. She is a Certified Health Coach, Certified Personal Trainer and PraiseMoves Instructor.

Judy's lifelong mission is to help individuals become fit and healthy through her businesses.

Joy to Go: The Elixir of Champions!, a devotional on joy, is her first book.

Judy lives in Connecticut with her husband, Ken.